General editor: Graham Handley M

Brodie's Notes on J. B. Priestley's

An Inspector Calls

P. Gooden BA
English Department, Kingswood School, Bath

Pan Books London, Sydney and Auckland

i

The excerpts from *An Inspector Calls* are reprinted by kind permission of the Trustees for the estate for the late J. B. Priestley

First published 1986 by Pan Books Ltd

This revised edition published 1991 by
Pan Books Ltd, Cavaye Place, London SW10 9PG

9 8 7 6 5 4 3 2 1

© Pan Books Ltd 1991

ISBN 0 330 50316 2

Photoset by Parker Typesetting Service, Leicester

Printed and bound in Great Britain by
Richard Clay Ltd, Bungay, Suffolk

Contents

These Notes are based on The Heinemann Educational edition of *An Inspector Calls* published in the Hereford Plays series but as each Act is analysed individually, the Notes may be used with any edition of the play.

Preface

The intention throughout this study aid is to stimulate and guide, to encourage your involvement in the book, and to develop informed responses and a sure understanding of the main details.

Brodie's Notes provide a clear outline of the play or novel's plot, followed by act, scene, or chapter summaries and/or commentaries. These are designed to emphasize the most important literary and factual details. Poems, stories or non-fiction texts combine brief summary with critical commentary on individual aspects or common features of the genre being examined. Textual notes define what is difficult or obscure and emphasize literary qualities. Revision questions are set at appropriate points to test your ability to appreciate the prescribed book and to write accurately and relevantly about it.

In addition, each of these Notes includes a critical appreciation of the author's art. This covers such major elements as characterization, style, structure, setting and themes. Poems are examined technically – rhyme, rhythm, for instance. In fact, any important aspect of the prescribed work will be evaluated. The aim is to send you back to the text you are studying.

Each study aid concludes with a series of general questions which require a detailed knowledge of the book: some of these questions may invite comparison with other books, some will be suitable for coursework exercises, and some could be adapted to work you are doing on another book or books. Each study aid has been adapted to meet the needs of the current examination requirements. They provide a basic, individual and imaginative response to the work being studied, and it is hoped that they will stimulate you to acquire disciplined reading habits and critical fluency.

Graham Handley 1990

The author and his work

John Boynton Priestley was born in Bradford in 1894. After service in World War I he went to Trinity Hall, Cambridge. He turned down the suggestion of a lectureship there after taking his degree and instead moved to London and a rather more precarious existence as a writer, unsupported by any institution. With a young family to provide for, Priestley turned his hand to different sorts of literary production. The variety of Priestley's output – essays and reviews, novels and plays, radio broadcasts and contributions to public life – may have been partly prompted by financial necessity in the early days of his life as a writer, but it equally reflects a width of taste and a desire to try his hand at as many different forms as possible.

His first success as a novelist was with *The Good Companions* (1929). Priestley was always drawn towards the theatre, however, and attached a special importance to that medium: 'If I wanted to make people feel deeply I should use the drama. You can create a quality of emotion in the theatre beyond any you can achieve in another medium,' he once said. His first play was *Dangerous Corner* (1932). Interestingly, it has a number of parallels with *An Inspector Calls*: both plays employ the same structural unities; both employ a kind of 'trick' of circularity whereby the play's ending seems about to lead us back to its beginning; and both are concerned with an investigation of what at first appears to be suicide but could more properly be termed murder. The later play, however, shows Priestley's development: the characters and dialogue are much more natural-seeming and the technical 'trick' exists not just for its own sake but is an integral part of the drama. *Dangerous Corner* was the first of many plays. Priestley was not content merely to produce the script on which the actors and director would operate. He became involved in every aspect of the production, directing and, on one occasion, acting. It is plain that the theatre exerted a kind of spell over him, and that he felt the excitement of an approaching first night as keenly as any actor. In his travel book *English Journey* (1934) Priestley describes his sensations at such a moment:

'The theatre gets you. The play binds you, body and soul. There seems to be nothing else worth talking about. If the papers announced that half a continent had been blown into the ocean, you would not spend five minutes talking or thinking about it . . . Only the people connected with the show and the theatre are real.'

Priestley's plays are variously comedies, pieces of social observation and criticism, and sometimes dramas which can be labelled 'experimental'. The latter category generally involves some manipulation of our normal understanding of the passing of time, a subject which always preoccupied Priestley. There is a trace of this in the circular construction of *An Inspector Calls* but the play – one of Priestley's most successful in audience terms – principally stands as a piece of social criticism.

In addition to his many plays and books on topics as diverse as music-halls or the relationship between man and time, Priestley also produced novels for most of his writing life, the best known of which are probably *The Good Companions* (1929) and *Angel Pavement* (1930). The very facility with which Priestley wrote – and wrote so much – has inevitably been turned against him. Suspicion was roused, too, by his 'hopping' (Priestley's own term) from one literary form to another. Being prolific and being versatile might also mean, to the hostile critic, being shallow and inadequate in any single literary form. Priestley was aware of – and sensitive to – these criticisms. Whatever the accuracy of some of the charges levelled against him, there can be little doubt that a fair proportion of Priestley's dramatic and fictional output will survive; it has, in any case, generally proved more popular with readers and audiences than it has with academic critics.

Priestley did not confine his activities to literature. After World War II he served as a delegate to a branch of the United Nations and he was later to play a part in the formative years of the Campaign for Nuclear Disarmament. He saw himself as having a social as well as a literary role; in this he was probably the last of a line of writers whose concerns were as much political and social as artistic. H.G. Wells and George Bernard Shaw – both mentioned disparagingly by Mr Birling in *An Inspector Calls* as examples of men over-concerned with society's problems – were earlier examples of the kind of public figure into which Priestley fashioned himself. J.B. Priestley continued to write and to speak out until the later years of his life. He died in August 1984.

Literary terms used in these notes

coup de théâtre A sudden turn of events in a drama.

euphemism An indirect word or expression used in place of a plainer one which might give rise to offence e.g. 'less than truthful' for 'lying'.

genre Literary type or category in books, plays, films, etc. Comedy, tragedy, farce are some of the dramatic genres.

Irony Irony is easier to detect in practice than it is to define. One (broad) definition would be that irony is the exploitation of the gap between the way things appear and the way they really are. In a drama, for instance, a character's plans may be frustrated by circumstances and recoil against him: in *Hamlet* one of the characters is mortally wounded by a poison-tipped sword that he intended to use against Hamlet himself. The audience perceives this situation as ironic – as does the character himself! Most irony is unperceived by the person who is its 'victim'; for example, a figure in a novel or a play might compliment himself or criticize others, but the reader or audience will be aware that the compliment is inappropriate (a coward might claim to be a brave man, like Falstaff in *Henry IV*) or that the criticism of others would be better applied to the speaker himself. In a play, irony is the means by which the playwright invites the audience into a kind of conspiracy with him because both the creator and the spectator know more about the situation than those who are enmeshed in it. An obvious example from *An Inspector Calls* is Birling's confident talk about the Titanic: we know what happened to the ship; he does not.

Realism True to life in artistic presentation. In a drama, realism is the attempt by the playwright to provide an accurate representation in terms of character, language, etc., of the world outside the theatre. Such an attempt involves in itself a good deal of artifice and any 'realistic' drama will be a selective and heightened mirroring of real life, however unstructured it appears on stage.

Act summaries, critical commentary, textual notes and revision questions

Act 1

The play opens in the dining-room of the Birling house. The family has just finished a meal in celebration of the engagement of Sheila Birling to Gerald Croft, son of another prosperous businessman in the imaginary city of 'Brumley'. The mood of the party is happy, even smug. Into this tight little household comes an Inspector Goole to announce an unpleasant suicide: a young woman has died in the Infirmary after swallowing disinfectant. It transpires that, under the name Eva Smith, she had been dismissed two years earlier from Birling's factory for being one of the ringleaders among workers agitating for a pay rise. The involvement of the family with the dead girl spreads as Sheila realizes, prompted by the Inspector's questions, that she was responsible for getting the young girl sacked from her next job as an assistant in a dress shop. Gerald Croft, too, appears startled when one of the names that the dead girl assumed is mentioned. Sheila urges him to be truthful about any links he may have had with Eva Smith, but Gerald imagines that these can be kept secret from the Inspector.

Commentary

This opening act shows the solid, careful construction which is one of Priestley's hallmarks as a dramatist. The foundation of our understanding of the characters is rapidly laid, the setting and the period are quickly established. In the following piece of dialogue, for example, from the play's first moments, a couple of character points are economically made:

Sheila You're squiffy.
Eric I'm not.
Mrs Birling What an expression, Sheila! Really, the things you girls pick up these days!

We learn later that Eric's 'squiffiness' (i.e. mild drunkenness) is a fairly constant feature of his behaviour, signifying something of the weakness and anxiety which mark his character. Mrs Birling's priggish response to her daughter's words above hints at the snobbish and conventional elements which play such a large part in her nature. Touches such as these help to 'fix' the characters for an audience so that when they are put to the test by the Inspector's visit their responses appear to proceed naturally and coherently out of what we already know about them. This is not to say that Priestley is incapable of providing some surprises in the development of his characters; for instance, the seemingly weak Eric ultimately shows a greater capacity to confront and accept responsibility for what has happened than an apparently stronger and more confident character such as Gerald. Whatever variations may follow, however, the outlines of character are laid down in Act 1.

Priestley has structured *An Inspector Calls* so that each act offers the audience a number of revelations and, although the general shape and direction of the play become evident by the end of the first act, the dramatist's ingenuity provides twists and surprises in the plot until the final curtain. In Act 1 two members of the Birling family are implicated in the death of Eva Smith. Arthur Birling has dismissed her as a trouble-maker at his factory: her offence was to go on strike for an increase in wages. Birling is presented, unsympathetically, as a no-nonsense employer determined to see that his interests (and those of his class) are properly protected. His workers are paid the average, no more, no less; agitators are kicked out. Birling has no reservations about his actions in the case of this particular girl, but his son Eric is mildly critical of his father's attitude.

More immediately, Sheila objects to the description of people like Eva Smith as 'cheap labour'. She has yet to learn of her own part in this chronological account of the girl's decline and death. However, the responses of son and daughter to the Inspector's news of the family's involvement stand in contrast to the hard-headed attitude of Birling and Gerald Croft, who confirms that in similar circumstances he too would have dismissed the girl. Sheila is presented as kinder and gentler than her father and, although her anger at Eva Smith's supposed 'impertinence' at the dress shop led to the latter's losing her job there as well, Sheila now acknowledges that she had felt guilty at the time and she miserably asks the Inspector, 'So I'm really responsible?' (for the girl's suicide). In this act, as in the other two, Sheila operates as the family 'conscience', a role in which she is supported by

Eric. She is the first to 'confess' her guilt at the beginning, just as she is the first at the play's end to fight against the complacent normality her family tries to wrap around itself. She is set against her father and her fiancé in their self-satisfaction and rejection of blame. Ironically at the end of Act 1, Gerald declines any responsibility in the girl's suicide but Sheila knows intuitively that the Inspector is aware of much which has not yet come to light. There are secrets still to be uncovered, and any character not yet implicated cannot afford to take a detached or nonchalant stance towards events.

Contrast is an essential feature of drama and Act 1 provides us with contrasts of character and of mood. In the first half of the act we see the Birling family in all its solid prosperity and self-righteousness. As the play proceeds we begin to realize that the basis for this prosperity and confidence is not well-founded. Priestley gives clear signals that the assurance, the self-congratulatory 'cosiness' of the Birlings, especially of the father, are going to be undermined by circumstances. Mr Birling tackles those who think that war is inevitable (remember that the play is set in 1912):

'And to that I say – fiddlesticks! The Germans don't want war. Nobody wants war . . . Everything to lose and nothing to gain by war.'

Progress, at least of the economic, material kind, is as certain as is the fact that the *Titanic* is unsinkable, again according to Birling. It would be easy to accuse Priestley of sneering with hindsight at the stupidity of some of his characters, for example when Birling, after citing the *Titanic* as evidence of irresistible human progress, goes on to say that within a few decades there will be no industrial strife and no wars; the triumph of progress will be complete.

The point about such a speech, in which history has made the speaker's predictions ridiculous, is that the optimism shown by Birling is blind and facile. The prosperity that he and his class demand and expect to occur automatically is won at the expense of other groups. For them the concept of human progress is diminished to the idea of machines or to the realization by employers that their interests must be more effectively protected.

Birling envisages a time some thirty or more years after the period in which the action of the play is set when 'all these Capital versus Labour agitators' will have been forgotten, but he offers no hint as to how this process will occur except through the employers' rightful (in his eyes) exercise of authority over their workers. At this level Act 1 – in fact, the play as a whole – does illustrate the operation of a kind of class warfare. Birling and Sheila make a victim out of Eva Smith, the one because she had the daring to ask for a bit more cash, the other because she had the cheek to smile behind the daughter's back. The result in both cases was the same: the unfortunate girl lost her job, because the father owns the factory and because the daughter had sufficient influence to oust a 'nobody' from her job. Having ruined the girl materially, the Birling family and others will go on to ruin her in different ways as Priestley strongly hints by the reaction of Gerald Croft at the end of Act 1.

The governor i.e. Gerald's father.

squiffy Mildly drunk.

It's one of the happiest nights of my life Birling's comment has an evident irony in view of everything that occurs later in the play.

lower costs and higher prices Birling states simply the creed that he follows in manufacturing: goods are to be produced at the lowest possible cost (in labour and materials) and sold to the consumer at the highest possible market price.

Steady the Buffs! The Buffs was a term used to describe a British army regiment, from the (light yellow) facings on the uniform. Eric's comment is a humorous appeal for self-control in his sister and her fiancé.

the interests of Capital 'Capital' is a collective term for the resources, including material and financial ones, used in the conducting of business. More broadly it can apply to those groups in a society who have control of property, money and resources. Arthur Birling employs the word in a commercial context and he is himself, of course, a representative of the 'capitalist' class.

the Kaiser The German Emperor, Kaiser Wilhelm II (1882–1941).

the Balkans Area of south-east Europe composed of various states and nationalities and scene of unrest and wars in the 19th and early 20th centuries.

You've a lot to learn yet Birling's remark is directed at Eric but applies ironically to the whole family, including himself.

the *Titanic* The giant passenger liner which sank in the Atlantic after striking an iceberg on her maiden voyage (April 14, 1912). Over 1500 lives were lost. Birling, like everybody else, considered the ship 'absolutely unsinkable'.

except of course in Russia . . . naturally Another comment by Birling which indicates his limited and ignorant view of the world. Five years after the time in which *An Inspector Calls* is set (1912) Russia was convulsed by the Revolution, and fresh in the audience's memory at the first London production of the play (1946) would be the fact of Russia's participation on the Allied side in World War II. Birling's patronizing remark would probably have been badly received.

Bernard Shaws and H.G. Wellses Bernard Shaw (1856–1950) was a dramatist and critic; H.G. Wells (1866–1946) a novelist, essayist and science-fiction writer. Both were social critics and theorists whose ideas would be the opposite of the narrow creed espoused by Birling.

landed people i.e. those owning large areas of land.

Honours List The annual publication of the names of those who have been awarded a decoration or a title for some services done (to the state, to politics, etc.) and who will be given their award by the monarch.

party man i.e. supporter of a political party.

a man has to make his own way ... to much harm Again, Birling's remarks are to be over-turned by the end of the evening.

on the Bench i.e. as a magistrate.

Well, I don't think it's very funny Eric's touchy response to the suggestion of the other two men that the policeman's visit might concern him indicates a scarcely hidden guilt and anxiety.

I was an alderman ... still on the Bench Birling's words here are a rather obvious attempt to impress the policeman with a catalogue indicating the speaker's social status and weight.

Still, I can't accept any responsibility Priestley's thesis in the play is that responsibility for others must be accepted, if not willingly then involuntarily.

public-school-and-Varsity Eric has been expensively educated at a private school and university. Despite this, his father claims he is not yet willing to face 'a few responsibilities', an ironic statement in view of the fact that Mr Birling has moments before disclaimed any responsibility for Eva Smith. In fact Birling's definition of responsibility would be 'self-interest'.

Go on the streets A euphemism for 'turn to prostitution'.

It was my own fault Contrast the directness of Sheila's assumption of blame in having the girl fired from the shop with her father's rejection of responsibility.

it's a bit thick i.e. a bit 'much' – Eric's way of expressing indignation at his sister's behaviour in the dress shop and her part in the chain of events that led to the girl's death.

he goes across to the tantalus A tantalus is a stand in which decanters are visible but under lock and key. Gerald Croft's movement signals his unease to the audience.

Were you seeing her last spring and summer ... were so busy? Sheila has caught the Inspector's appetite for the truth. Having 'confessed' herself she now feels that everyone else must be equally straightforward. She also shares something of the Inspector's sense of whether someone is telling the truth or not.

Revision questions on Act 1

1 What impression do we receive of the Birling household before the Inspector arrives?

2 What do the historical references – particularly those made by Mr Birling – contribute to Act 1?

3 Describe the similarities and the differences in the treatment given to Eva Smith by Mr Birling and by his daughter.

4 Describe the character of Gerald Croft, giving an account of any development of it in the course of Act 1.

5 Discuss some examples of irony in Act 1.

Act 2

The distance between Sheila and Gerald Croft widens when he suggests that his fiancé's wish to be present at the Inspector's questioning of him springs from her desire to see him suffer. She is repelled by this assessment of her. Mr and Mrs Birling reappear. Gerald eventually reveals that he knew Eva Smith under the name of Daisy Renton. He met her when she was hard-up and hungry and had soon installed her as his mistress in a vacant flat. The affair was over by the end of the summer. The next member of the household into whose hands the girl fell was Mrs Birling; an important member of the Brumley Women's Charity Organization, she had been outraged when Eva Smith has asked for help from her committee, taking the name of 'Mrs Birling'. The girl was pregnant but refused to marry the father of her child because she regarded him as immature; she also refused to accept any of the man's money because she believed it to be stolen. The real Mrs Birling gives vent to her moral indignation: the girl was a liar, not a deserving case, etc. She blames the unknown young father who, she feels, must be made to acknowledge in public his responsibility and then be dealt with by the Inspector. She continues in this vein until it slowly dawns on her that the man in question is her son Eric. As he enters, the curtain comes down for the end of Act 2.

Commentary

Act 2 follows the pattern set in the first act. Two more characters – Gerald Croft and Mrs Birling – come under the Inspector's scrutiny; as in the first part of the play, one of them is receptive to what the Inspector says while the other is not. Croft appears the less blameworthy. When he first met the girl in the music-hall he was attracted to her but he also felt sorry for her. He claims that pity and not any ulterior motive made him provide her with a vacant flat belonging to a friend of his. Although he is defending himself here by presenting his behaviour in the best light, Croft is the first character to have offered the girl kindness and shelter instead of coldness and rejection; the girl's response arises naturally from her loneliness and gratitude. Although Croft finally drops her she remains almost pathetically thankful for what he has done, keeping 'a rough sort of diary "just to make it last longer" ', as the Inspector tells them.

In contrast Mrs Birling continues to defend herself even after it is revealed that she turned the pregnant girl away from her 'charity' organization. She echoes her husband's reaction in Act 1 when she states that her actions were justified. Mrs Birling was prejudiced by the girl's impudence in using the family name and she believes that the absent father should be compelled to take responsibility for the girl's support. There is, of course, an ironic aptness in Eva Smith's having taken the Birling surname, just as there is in Mrs Birling's directions to the Inspector to go in search of the absent father. Mrs Birling not only condemns herself out of her own mouth – 'charity organization' is plainly an ironic misnomer – but she condemns others in her family too in suggesting that the Inspector's time would be better spent in fastening blame where it really belongs (i.e. on her son) just as she had earlier made a much worse condemnation in shutting out the girl who was carrying what would have been her grandchild. That condemnation was a kind of inadvertent death sentence.

An unpleasant snobbery, too, enters into Mrs Birling's coldness: 'I don't suppose for a moment that we can understand why the girl committed suicide. Girls of that class – ' she says before being interrupted by Sheila and before the truth about her own involvement is revealed. Again, the mother claims that the girl's story to the charity committee showed 'elaborate fine feelings and scruples that were simply absurd in a girl in her position'. But here as well Mrs Birling's words rebound on her. It was Eva Smith who displayed genuinely fine feelings – tact, delicacy, a relative honesty – both in her attempt to protect Eric (she does not name him to his mother) and in her refusal of his assistance because she believed Eric had stolen the money.

The pretensions of the Birlings to be somehow 'better' or more deserving than others are dramatically shown to be false. Mr and Mrs Birling are the least sympathetic figures in the play. Neither is capable of responding in anything other than an unfeeling and selfish way to the girl's death, even when the extent of their involvement is forced upon them by the Inspector. They are either ignorant or dismissive of those 'beneath' them in a social order which operates to their advantage. They are worried only about preserving a respectable facade and the threat posed by a scandal. Neither is able to react in a way which would make him or her, even momentarily, attractive to the audience. In this they provide a contrast with the younger characters who are much more affected by the Inspector's call.

As the Inspector's questions to the family demonstrate its inescapable involvement with the death of Eva Smith, it is the younger characters who show the capacity for a proper response while the older ones are fixed in their moulds of resentment and evasion. Sheila advises her mother that she 'mustn't try to build up a kind of wall between us and that girl'; she appreciates Gerald's new-found honesty as he talks about his relationship with the girl; she announces that what has been revealed has changed them. Gerald also has the sensitivity to be upset and disturbed by the news, even if only temporarily. The knowledge each member of the family has of the others is being added to by the 'confessions', and as knowledge grows so do relationships between individuals change. Priestley is concerned to dramatize not just the impact of the suicide on one character after another but also to show how changed feelings and judgements lead to reassessments within the group.

In Act 2 Priestley also touches on the subject of sexual hypocrisy. The male characters are adept at applying double standards: women within their family or social circle are to be treated one way, women outside the circle (particularly those of a lower class) may be approached differently. Gerald Croft is at first concerned to prevent his fiancé from hearing of his affair with Daisy Renton. Mr Birling similarly wants to protect his daughter from having to hear about the 'women of the town'. Such talk is for male ears only, not for respectable ladies, but the Inspector points out, 'Your daughter isn't living on the moon. She's here in Brumley too.' It must be remembered that Priestley is depicting a period and a society that was repressed and sensitive about sexual matters in comparison to our own or to the time of the play's first production (mid 1940s). But the more general point which the dramatist is making remains valid: that outward respectability is no guide to inner worth, that it may in fact conceal a lack of charity or even an active corruption. The upholders of the status quo may have more to be ashamed of than those who apparently flout it. Gerald casually mentions that he 'rescued' the girl in the bar from the drunken and unwelcome attentions of one of Mr Birling's fellow aldermen, 'one of the worst sots and rogues in Brumley'.

Like the opening Act of *An Inspector Calls*, the second scrapes off the veneer of responsibility and conformism from the lives of the reputable members of a community. Where Act 1 had dealt with the material ruin of Eva Smith, the remaining two acts outline her 'moral' ruin at the hands of those members of the town who regard themselves as upholders and enforcers of public morality.

Yes, but you don't believe me . . . believe me Sheila's comment indicates her disappointment that honesty and mutual trust do not characterize her relationship with Gerald at this moment of greatest strain.

You see, we have to share . . . our guilt The Inspector's bleak comment summarizes an important aspect of the play. The society depicted by Priestley shares out its goods very unequally but the class represented by the Birlings, although wanting the larger portion of material goods for itself, refuses to take much (any?) share of responsibility for others less fortunate. Something has to be shared, however, and if responsibility fails then it will be blame that is handed out.

She goes closer to him, wonderingly The movement signifies the beginning of Sheila's doubts about the 'identity' of the Inspector.

it seems to me that we have more reason for taking offence Mrs Birling, always on the look-out for any slight to herself or her social status, easily 'takes offence'. The Inspector gives the conventional phrase a different and threatening meaning by the emphasis of his reply, 'Let's leave *offence* out of it, shall we?' The offence has already been committed *by* the Birling family rather than *against* them.

You know of course . . . two years ago Mrs Birling makes as unsubtle an attempt as that of her husband to impress the Inspector. In fact, the couple's assertions of their position in the community ironically underline their failures of responsibility in their dealings with Eva Smith.

But we really must stop . . . isn't used to drink Sheila's urge to conceal nothing from the Inspector springs in part from her belief that he knows much already and in part from her new-found desire for directness and honesty in family discussion.

I don't propose to give you much more rope i.e. Birling does not intend to grant Goole freedom of action to pursue his inquiries for much longer. Sheila alone realizes that the reverse is the truth: the Inspector is giving them rope 'so that we'll hang ourselves'.

women of the town Prostitutes.

you're forgetting I'm supposed to be engaged to the hero of it Sheila's reply to her mother is a rebuke – she has a natural interest in hearing what Gerald has been doing despite Mrs Birling's alarm that the story might be 'unsuitable' for her daughter's ears. 'Hero' would be delivered ironically or sarcastically: Gerald looks likely to appear in anything but the 'heroic' light that Sheila has presumably been accustomed to see him by.

she wanted to be Daisy Renton – and not Eva Smith Priestley has two reasons for changing the girl's name: it reflects her desire as a character to make a fresh start after her disastrous experiences in work; also it enables Priestley to withhold until the end of Act 1 the revelation of Gerald's involvement with her, as he recognizes her only under her assumed name and not her real one.

didn't like the idea of her going back to the Palace bar The implication of Gerald's remark is that the alternative to his installing the girl as his mistress was for her to slip into a life of prostitution.

didn't want to take any more from me Another mark of the girl's scrupulousness: she is uneasy at accepting Gerald's money.

And now at least you've been honest Sheila's comments here point towards her different attitude to Gerald Croft. She no longer wants to remain engaged to him; at the very least, they will have to establish their relationship on a new footing.

You were in the chair i.e. Mr Birling was presiding over the meeting.

It didn't take me long to get the truth ... out of her Mrs Birling takes pleasure in her ability to see through others: it did not take her long to penetrate the falsity of the girl's story (though it was, in all essentials, true). It is ironic that her remark here could be applied to the Inspector and his effect on the family.

she seemed to me to be not a good case i.e the girl calling herself Mrs Birling did not appear to be a suitable object for charity. In fact she ('alone, friendless', etc.) was above all a charitable case but the real Mrs Birling's prejudice and snobbery resulted in her being turned down by the committee.

As if a girl of that sort would ever refuse money! We already know from Gerald Croft's testimony that the girl turned down his offer of more money.

some drunken young idler Ironically, Mrs Birling characterizes her son more truly than she knows!

SHEILA (*with sudden alarm*): Mother – stop – stop! With her usual quick intuition Sheila is the first to see the identity of the young man her mother is so severely condemning.

MRS BIRLING (*agitated*): I don't believe it. I *won't* believe it ... For Mrs Birling belief is an act of will; this enables her to ignore facts which she finds unpalatable.

Revision questions on Act 2

1 Describe the change that occurs in the relationship between Sheila and Gerald Croft in the course of Act 2.

2 Would you agree that Mrs Birling is presented as an absolutely unsympathetic character in this Act?

3 Describe, with reference and quotation, the stages in Eva Smith's life as revealed in Act 2.

4 Describe and discuss the dramatic surprises produced by the author in Act 2.

5 What do we learn about Brumley and its inhabitants in this Act?

Act 3

Eric, the Birlings' son, appears at the beginning of the act and his connection with the dead girl is soon established. He made her pregnant but, despite this, she did not want to marry him. Eric provided her with money he had 'borrowed' from his father's office until the girl refused to accept any further gifts of money from him. It was after this that she presented herself to Mrs Birling's charity committee, only to be rejected. The Inspector's investigation of the household is over. He has forced on them the unwelcome knowledge that each played a part in bringing Eva Smith to her death. He leaves the house. At once there is an outburst of recrimination, children and parents turning on each other. Then doubt: there was something 'curious' about the Inspector. Was he a genuine policeman? The older Birlings begin to regain their balance and with it their capacity for indignation. Gerald Croft returns from a walk outside, having discovered that there is no Inspector Goole on the local force, a fact confirmed by Birling's call to the Chief Constable. The family, led by the father and by Gerald Croft, argue themselves out of any complicity in the girl's death. A call to the Infirmary establishes that there has been no suicide for months. Sheila and Eric insist that this makes no difference to the essential truth of the Inspector's accusations and the validity of the family's confessions, but the others are impatient with them and gleeful at their escape from scandal. At that moment the telephone rings: a police inspector is on his way to the Birling house to ask some questions about the suicide of a girl who has just died on the way to the Infirmary. The play ends.

Commentary

The final Act takes the Birling family through several changes of mood. The confession of Eric at the beginning completes the pattern of the family's involvement with the dead girl. His behaviour towards her is presented as selfish, immature and unscrupulous. Again, the girl is shown as having had finer feelings and a greater sense of moral responsibility than any of the family who dragged her down. She rejects Eric's suggestion of marriage because she perceives that he doesn't love her; finally she will not see him again because he has been stealing money to give to her. Perhaps this last detail is implausible — without knowing more about the situation, it is a little hard to believe that Eva Smith, pregnant, friendless, etc., would so adamantly turn down help from someone who is both responsible in part for her plight and also patently better off than she is herself. This is not, however, the kind of consideration that would occur to an audience as it was actually experiencing the play, and it suits Priestley's dramatic purposes to present the girl as the innocent and principled victim of the Birling's selfish abuse. Her good qualities make her death more shocking and show up more sharply the hypocrisy of her persecutors, particularly that of the Birling parents.

The Inspector's recapitulation of the 'charges' against the family makes the guilt both individual and communal: Mrs Birling turned away the girl who was pregnant with her own grandchild (a final and distressing irony); Eric had 'used her for the end of a stupid drunken evening, as if she was an animal, a thing, not a person'; Sheila had had her dismissed while the father had started the whole process by firing her from his factory. The least culpable, in the Inspector's eyes, is Gerald Croft who was fond of her and had succeeded in making her happy for a while. Each character has touched the life of Eva Smith at some point in her decline, and touched it for the worse, so that this victim of the Birling family has received from each encounter a fresh impetus on the road to self-destruction.

Nothing more can be done for Eva Smith. But the Inspector uses what the family has learnt — or should have learnt — from his visit to point a moral: 'but there are millions and millions and millions of Eva Smiths and John Smiths still left with us ... all intertwined with our lives, with what we think and say and do. We don't live alone. We are members of one body.' (See under

Themes for further discussion of this passage). Dramatic interest now centres on what the characters have discovered about themselves and each other and what they have been taught. Mrs Birling is perhaps the least affected: Mr Birling is most concerned by the damage that will be done to his reputation and the effect of the scandal on his chances of a knighthood – this apart, the most alarming and insulting bit of news for him is that his son has stolen from his own business. For Sheila and, to a lesser extent, for Eric, the Inspector's call has altered their lives irrevocably, just as their own thoughtlessness altered the life of Eva Smith. Sheila is horrified that her parents have not learned a lesson from the tragedy.

Priestley provides us with two more narrative twists. The first is the discovery that Inspector Goole was probably a fake; Birling puts the whole thing down to a hoax played by some personal enemy. This lets the family off the hook. They are free to resume their normal lives as if nothing has happened because, if there is no genuine police interest in the case, there is no danger of public exposure. The younger Birlings, however, do not respond with sighs of relief but with expressions of dismay at the attitudes of the parents and Gerald:

Birling This makes a difference, y'know. In fact, it makes all the difference.
Gerald Of course!
Sheila (*bitterly*) I suppose we're all nice people now.

For the Birling children it is the facts that are significant and shaming for the family; for the others it is not the facts that matter but the danger of their becoming public property and raising a scandal. Having averted this danger, as they think, they now try to shed the last vestige of moral responsibility for the suicide. Instead of an open acknowledgment of their roles in it, they resort to evasion in the search for an exit from guilt. Perhaps there were several different girls rather than the one claimed by the Inspector? Has each member of the family confessed to an involvement with someone different? If so, the guilt would be so diluted that any pangs of conscience would be easily appeased. Only Sheila and Eric remain convinced of their responsibility in the girl's suicide.

For the whole family relief comes after the call to the Infirmary (confirming that there has been no suicide for a long time). Still Sheila and her brother are dissenting voices, treating the whole business as a warning. It is an event which has made her look at herself and her family in a different and harsher light. For the others normality is restored; they pretend to be 'amused' by what has obviously been an elaborate hoax; Gerald offers the engagement ring again to Sheila, whose wariness over accepting it contrasts with her eagerness to take it in Act 1.

The final twist in the plot is provided by the play's closing moment. The telephone call to announce a police inspector's imminent arrival throws the Birlings back into the morass of guilt and confusion from which they have just so laboriously extricated themselves. It is also a highly effective theatrical moment and makes us hurriedly review our understanding of one of the principal characters: Inspector Goole. At first a genuine (if unusual) policeman, then an apparent sham, he now appears – in retrospect – as an altogether more sinister and omniscient figure. It is the kind of ending likely to send an audience out of the theatre satisfied because a dramatic pattern has been completed – the play ending more or less where it began (see under *Dramatic structure* for a fuller discussion of this topic) – and because it offers room for speculation and discussion for members of that audience.

take your mother along to the drawing-room Birling's direction to Sheila indicates his continuing desire to prevent the women in the family from hearing anything unsavoury, in this case the details of Eric's affair with the girl.

I hate these fat old tarts round the town – the ones I see some of your respectable friends with This scornful remark from Eric again hints at the double standards applied in sexual matters and at the hypocrisy of some of the leading members of the community.

I've got to cover this up as soon as I can Birling's instinctive response to his son's confession that he has stolen from the family business is indicative of his approach to anything that threatens the reputation of his family.

Your trouble is – you've been spoilt Birling's accusation is of course ironic; he and, more particularly, Mrs Birling, have been doing the 'spoiling'.

then they will be taught it in fire and blood and anguish The Inspector's warning, in the context of the play's period, must be seen to apply to the outbreak of World War I, but his comment has a general validity: that the alternative to the harmony and interdependence which he advocates is bitterness and war.

Apparently nothing matters to you Again, Birling's words have an ironic reference to himself; nothing is of any significance to him except the prospect of being deprived of his knighthood because of a scandal.

Eric, I'm absolutely ashamed of you Similarly, Mrs Birling's attack on her son shows that she has learnt little or nothing; she has as much to be ashamed of as he has.

He was our police inspector all right Eric means that questions about the authenticity of the Inspector are irrelevant. As far as the Birling family was concerned, he 'inspected' them (their stories, their motives, their excuses, etc.) with all the authority and hard attention of a genuine officer.

Probably a Socialist or some sort of crank – he talked like one By bracketing the Inspector with a group naturally hostile to men like himself, Birling is able to account for his prejudice and hostility and so reduce the impact of the Inspector's attack.

You see, Gerald, you haven't to know the rest of our crimes and idiocies Already the family is closing up round its secrets; the Birlings want to conceal Eric's misdeeds from Gerald even though he insisted, in Act 1, on being 'one of the family'.

BIRLING: Look – for God's sake!

MRS BIRLING (*protesting*): Arthur! Mrs Birling's shock at her husband's oath is another ironic comment on her scale of values. That he should swear is rather more outrageous to her than most of the evening's revelations.

there's still no proof it was really the same girl The Birling parents and Croft spend time and ingenuity working out the way in which they have been 'tricked' by the Inspector. In fact, the elaborate contrivances of substituted photographs and of an imposter presenting herself to the charity committee are inherently less likely than the straightforward story recounted by the Inspector but they desperately need to find some way to explain away the life history of Eva Smith so that it ceases to be real and their responsibility.

BIRLING (*uneasily*): It will look a bit queer, won't it – ringing up at this time of night – Gerald's confidence that the whole affair was a hoax is not yet absolutely shared by Birling. His unwillingness to contact the Infirmary springs from a fear that the complicated barrier they have erected against the truth may be broken down by any communication with an incontrovertible source of information in the world outside.

a lot of moonshine A lot of nonsense.

an elaborate sell A clever piece of deception.

In the morning they'll be as amused as we are Mrs Birling's prediction is about to be proved wrong. In fact none of them is really 'amused', but the alternative to treating what has occurred as a joke is to take it seriously, and this is unacceptable.

What about this ring? Gerald wants to restore his former relationship with Sheila too easily. He repeats the presentation made at the beginning of the play, but other events are about to repeat themselves also.

the famous younger generation who know it all Birling's sneer works against himself: his children do, in a sense, 'know' more than their parents. They have acquired some self-knowledge in the course of the evening as well as a bleaker, more realistic view of the family.

Revision questions on Act 3

1 What changes are there in Eric's character in the course of this Act?

2 What relevance has the Inspector's final warning in his last speech to the story of Eva Smith?

3 Describe the way in which the Birling family gradually come to believe that the Inspector is not a genuine policeman.

4 Contrast the attitudes of Sheila and Mrs Birling in the second half of Act 3.

5 What is the impact of the telephone call at the very end of the play?

Priestley's art
in *An Inspector Calls*

The characters

Priestley's characterization in *An Inspector Calls* is adequate for the purposes of plot and theme. No one character is concentrated on or developed at the expense of others. It would be difficult to claim that any figure on stage fitted the description 'central character' unless it is, paradoxically, the dead girl whose very absence dominates all the events of the play. Priestley also relies to an extent on stock 'types' in this play: the hard-headed businessman with little time for anything outside work, family and respectability; the daughter, more impulsive and spontaneous than her parents, ready to question their values, etc. The familiarity of such types for an audience enables the playwright to sketch in the outlines of characters without having to provide the colouring or detail which would slow down the action. In any case, one of the points Priestley is making is that the guilt of the Birlings is communal as well as individual. The Inspector's attention turns from one individual to another for a few minutes of stage-time; to develop one character by exploring motive and response more fully would be to distort the pattern and dramatic movement of the play. Although Priestley shows considerably greater insight into his characters than, say, an Agatha Christie there is a similarity between the range and type of figures presented in *An Inspector Calls* and a 'whodunnit' melodrama. This is appropriate when one considers that the author is also interested in establishing responsibility for a death which can in effect be regarded as 'murder' by a group of people.

Mr Birling

hard-headed, practical

He is a successful man of business with a touch of smugness. He is very satisfied with the way in which he has risen in the world and sees himself as the best defender of his own interests and those of his class (i.e. the prosperous, the employers and factory owners). Business is, for Arthur Birling, entirely a matter of profit and loss, of ensuring that he gets his materials (including the people in his labour force) as cheaply as possible and sells the finished products for as high a price as the market will bear. Birling views the world from his side of the fence and makes a virtue of his limited view, turning it into what he regards as a more than adequate philosophy of life: 'a man has to make his own way – has to look after himself – and his family too, of course, when he has one – and so long as he does that he won't come to much harm.' In the same way he transforms his desire to make profits into a kind of moral obligation. He can show ruthlessness in ensuring that everything – and everyone – is subordinated to the overriding need for profitability. After the failed strike at his works he allows the strikers to return, at the old rates, but sacks the ring-leaders. His toughness and insensitivity become virtuous necessities in his eyes and Priestley is at pains to establish that he is an average employer paying average wages; there is nothing particularly bad or wicked about Birling. There is no suggestion that he enjoys 'punishing' those workers who have had the daring to request a rise in wages. It is rather that his sympathies are so narrow and his dedication to an arid concept of business so complete that his character is never adequate to meet the challenge or trial posed by the Inspector.

There are other layers in Birling's complacency: an overconfidence in progress which he believes must come because it suits *him* (he rejects predictions and fears of war because there is too much at stake for him). He is also buoyed up by the belief that he will find his way into the next Honours List. He says with studied arrogance: 'Just a knighthood, of course.' Later the prospect of being denied this honour because of the scandal causes him more anguish than anything else. Birling is proud of his present status in the community as prosperous businessman, ex-Lord Mayor, magistrate, etc., although he is uneasily aware in the presence of Gerald Croft that the young man comes of a 'better' family which might resent their son's marriage into his. Birling is a pillar of society, one of the upholders of community order and morality, but, Priestley suggests, he is hollow. His first response to the Inspector is crudely to affirm his social position and by so doing to put the policeman in *his*. Birling takes refuge behind his business commitments and his standing in the town, and disclaims any responsibility for what happened to the girl.

His desire to protect his family, mentioned earlier in the play, is critically examined by Priestley and found lacking. It emerges in the wish to prevent his daughter hearing anything 'indelicate'. This is an ironic and misplaced kind of tact; as Sheila points out, 'you're forgetting I'm supposed to be engaged to the hero of it' (i.e. the story that Gerald is about to tell). In fact, in any real crisis Birling is ineffectual or unapproachable, as Eric indicates at one point to his father's displeasure. Birling's response to the disaster that threatens to overwhelm his family is to defend himself, to attack others, or to assess the chances of covering up the whole affair.

Birling makes strenuous efforts to limit the damage to himself and his family but he can only do so by distorting or minimizing the truth so that the life of the household can be returned to its even, hypocritical keel. The final telephone call destroys all his efforts and threatens again the exposure of a weak and selfish character.

Mrs Birling

a rather cold woman and her husband's social superior

Essentially a character from the same mould as her husband, she has dedicated herself to his rise in society and evidently respects his achievement. At the end of the play, Mrs Birling again shows her dependence on him when she says to Sheila: 'Now just be quiet so that your father can decide what we ought to do.' If anything she is harder, more dismissive than Birling and she shows a greater capacity for outrage at a hint of the unrespectable; she is quick to detect rudeness, gross impertinence, the intention to cause offence in others and is always on the look-out for some insult to herself or to the family name. At the same time she is imperceptive about those around her or perhaps she is merely closing her eyes to what she does not wish to know. The Inspector asks of Eric, 'Isn't he used to drinking?'; Mrs Birling replies, 'No, of course not. He's only a boy.' Similarly she appears genuinely shocked by the information that another 'respected' community member is reputed to be a drunk.

Mrs Birling does not like anything that contradicts her reassuring image of the world around her. The revelation that the Inspector brings to her — that she indirectly helped to kill the girl bearing her own grandchild — is too painful for her to acknowledge or contemplate and she retreats behind protestations that she had only done her 'duty' (although the word actually means nothing to her and is only part of a self-defensive formula). She rapidly rounds on the others after Goole's departure and, recovering her self-possession, she accuses them of showing less coolness and firmness than herself. Priestley demonstrates that she will no more willingly change herself or her behaviour than will her husband.

Sheila Birling

a pretty girl in her early twenties, very pleased with life

The daughter of the Birling household, she is in effect the only character in *An Inspector Calls* to give an optimistic note to what is otherwise a fairly pessimistic drama. Some of her responses are echoed by Eric but Sheila is the stronger, more attractive character of the two. A figure like her – youthful, spontaneous, relatively honest and unselfish – is to be found in other Priestley plays. In part it is her youth which makes her more susceptible to what the Inspector is saying, but her temperament too is more engaging than the rest of the Birlings'. She lacks her parents' cold adherence to convention and respectability; she is more balanced, less evasive than her brother Eric. She has no doubt about the wrongness of the family's complicity in Eva Smith's death. When the Inspector leaves the stage it is Sheila who continues to articulate his – and the audience's – objections to the Birlings' attempts to resume a normal family life as if nothing had happened. Sheila is shown as having a quicker, more intuitive understanding than the others. She realizes it is useless to try to hide anything from Inspector Goole. She cautions her mother not 'to build up a kind of wall between us and that girl' because she sees the need for absolute honesty from each member of her family and from Gerald Croft. The same need for honesty in this situation *now* makes her applaud Gerald's confession.

A desire for frankness makes Sheila blurt out in front of the Inspector that Eric has a weakness for drink or claim that she wants to hear more detail about her fiancé's affair with the dead girl. For breaking ranks with the rest of her family in this way she is accused by her father of lacking a sense of loyalty, but the 'loyalty' she is being asked to maintain is an adherence to lies and half-truths, and ignores the larger loyalty, which the play as a whole urges upon us, to community and society. If Sheila has been deficient in this sort of larger loyalty in the past, the obvious implication of the changes that take place in her character during the course of the play is that she will be more attentive to wider responsibilities in the future.

While the energies of the other characters are devoted to concealing, Sheila's are dedicated to uncovering what they want to hide. It is important to see that this is not done in a malicious, vindictive spirit. In her determination to get at the truth Sheila becomes a kind of ally to the Inspector. In her reaction to his presence she is the first to suspect something out of the ordinary in him and the first to ask the question, '*was* he really a police inspector?' But her quickness and intuition are not used to shore up the family defences. She also understands that the question of the authenticity of the Inspector is not the important one. What matters is what each member of the household has revealed about him or herself. In her view – and it is one that Priestley implicitly endorses – they must all learn something from the experience and adjust their attitudes and behaviour accordingly. She shows some capacity to be changed by what she has done and seen; the rest, Eric apart, do not.

Sheila identifies herself with the dead girl: they were the same age, both were pretty, both were spirited and principled. She has an instinctive sympathy with anyone less fortunate than herself – 'But these girls aren't cheap labour – they're *people*', she says in objection to her father's definition of his factory workers. Before she knows of her own dealings with Eva Smith she describes the story of the girl's dismissal from Birling's firm and her subsequent impoverishment as 'a rotten shame'. She has no case to make against the society of which she is a secure and comfortable member but she has a ready imagination which enables her to identify herself with those who become that society's 'victims'.

Her character, however, must not be idealized, even if she does stand out from the remainder of her family. Of all the motives behind the humiliation and decline of Eva Smith, Sheila's was probably the most petty and, in some ways, the least excusable. She assumed that the girl had been impertinent in the dress shop by smiling 'as if to say: "Doesn't she look awful."' (Notice how Priestley minimizes any suggestion of rudeness on the girl's part to a mere look not intended to be seen by the

customer.) It is clear that Sheila's real objections to the girl
spring from jealousy: the dress that Sheila looked ridiculous in
suited Eva Smith, as Sheila is quick to acknowledge:

'If she'd been some miserable plain little creature, I don't suppose I'd
have done it. But she was very pretty and looked as if she could take
care of herself. I couldn't be sorry for her.'

Irritation and impatience provoke Sheila to make a complaint
about the girl's behaviour, something she felt uneasy about at
the time and something which she now bitterly regrets. Sheila
too, like the rest of the Birlings, tries to provide some excuses for
her behaviour. However, it is finally her honesty and willingness
to review her life, if necessary to change, that redeem Sheila just
as it is the absence of those qualities that condemns others.

Eric Birling

not quite at ease, half assertive

Part of Eric Birling's function in the play is to echo the attitude
and responses of his sister, but Priestley makes him a less open,
less attractive figure to us. He does not play much part in Acts 1
and 2, although he is a goad to his father's complacent opinions.
'What about war?' he asks as Birling talks about the inevitability
of a 'time of steadily increasing prosperity'. 'Why shouldn't they
try for higher wages?' he says of the strikers at his father's
factory. Such interjections do not go to make up a sustained case
against his family's way of life, and Eric is certainly no defender
of the downtrodden or the outcast, as his treatment of Eva Smith
demonstrates. A lot of what he says and does springs from
hostility to his parents, particularly to his father. He tries to slip
away when he discovers that the Inspector might want to question him too. When he finally comes to make his 'confession'
about his part in the suicide (Act 3) he emerges as an unimpress-
ive, weak figure. After his first meeting with Eva Smith he
returned with her to her lodgings. Later, on discovering that the
girl was pregnant he took money from his father's office to
support her, although he claims that this was merely borrowed
and not stolen. The girl, however, rejects Eric and the idea of
marriage to him. In the son's favour is the frankness with which
he at last talks about the whole affair. In the end he is willing to
look at it unblinkingly – 'the fact remains that I did what I did'.
Concealment and excuse no longer matter to him. In this he

joins Sheila in a kind of partnership which sets the two children against their parents.

Gerald Croft

very much the easy well-bred young man-about-town

The fiancé of Sheila Birling is, as her father is well aware, the social superior of the family into which he is marrying. His father 'Sir George' owns a business larger and older than Birling and Company as well as in friendly rivalry with it. As the inheritor of the business he finds himself a natural ally of the Birling father: he approves of the peremptory way in which Eva Smith was fired; he offers no dissenting voice to his prospective father-in-law's easy and consoling view of progress. His first response to the girl's death is to distance himself from it. He pleads with Sheila not to say anything about it to the Inspector after she has seen through his pretence of non-involvement. Finally driven to explain his liaison with the girl, however, he shows a capacity for a spontaneous human reaction which is denied to the other Birlings:

Gerald (distressed) Sorry – I – well, I've suddenly realised – taken it in properly – that she's dead –'

Croft presents himself as the girl's rescuer and although there in an element of self-justification in this both the Inspector and Sheila concede that there was some genuine feeling in him for Daisy Renton and that he at least made her happy for a time. Gerald Croft may be incapable of breaking out of a conventional mode of thought which endorses the existing social structure, but he appears as a more sympathetic figure than the Birling parents, even though he thinks as they do. This is partly because he is more properly responsive to the death and partly because he does not appear so preoccupied with social status or so fearful of scandal.

As the least culpable character, Gerald is the calmest in assessing the genuineness of their policeman visitor and in working out the way in which the family has been 'tricked' into believing the Inspector. He is the first to suggest that each member of the family may have been involved with a different girl rather than the same one, so offering a method of diffusing rather than concentrating blame. He has the least to lose if the scandal becomes public and he has a natural confidence and command which enable him to suggest ways in which the Birlings can salve their guilt by finding excuses. Gerald's interest in finding out the truth about the Inspector plainly springs from a desire to do a service for the Birlings and so restore himself in Sheila's eyes by redeeming his dishonesty towards her. He has an easy – perhaps rather glib – frankness:

'I did keep a girl last summer. I've admitted it. And I'm sorry, Sheila.'

Finally (and prematurely) he proclaims that all is well and offers Sheila the engagement ring again. It is evident that he falls into that category of characters who have learnt little or nothing from the experience which they have just endured and who believe life can be restored to normal after what is no more than a little 'upset'.

Inspector Goole

. . . has a disconcerting habit of looking hard at the person he addresses before actually speaking

An intentionally mysterious figure whose name is presumably meant to recall by its sound the term for an evil spirit, 'ghoul'. Certainly he comes to trouble the Birling household and it would be possible to see him as a representative of the dead girl, returned to earth in spirit form to 'haunt' the consciences of those who have procured her death. Priestley, however, does not intend one specific 'identity' to be given to the Inspector. He is the one character in the play who speaks with consistent moral force and assurance. The playwright explains in his stage directions that he must create 'at once an impression of massiveness, solidity and purposefulness'. For the first few minutes of his appearance on stage he seems to be making routine inquiries into the death of a girl. That the scope of his investigation is somewhat wider can be seen from the exchange with Mr Birling when the Inspector asks why the businessman refused to pay the striking workers the rise which they were demanding. Birling is taken aback: the Inspector is touching on a matter which Birling sees only as a private commercial consideration. The questions which Goole claims it is his duty to ask are directed to an examination not merely of the Birlings' involvement in the death of an individual but also of their belief that they lead responsible and worthwhile lives as members of society.

The Inspector has a number of functions in the play. He leads us

– and the characters – through a chronological account of Eva Smith's life, filling in the background detail for the periods when the Birlings were not involved with her decline: for example, 'She was out of work for the next two months. Both her parents were dead, so that she'd no home to go back to.' He acts as a kind of interrogator-cum-confessor to the household. Once each character has begun to talk about his or her connection with Eva Smith it requires only a prompt or a command from the Inspector for him to continue. There is, in this Inspector, a moral weight and an impression of great knowledge which make each of the 'wrongdoers' understand, at least for a time, that concealment is useless or wrong. As well as being the law he is obviously accustomed to laying down the law. It is an ethical rather than a criminal one: he suggests that Birling does not pay his employees much above subsistence level; he offers an interpretation of some inescapable moral principle: 'You see, we have to share something. If there's nothing else, we'll have to share our guilt' or, 'Public men, Mr Birling, have responsibilities as well as privileges.' The fact that the family make little objection to these statements of principle indicates that they recognize both the authority of the Inspector to make them and that he is correct in so saying.

Inspector Goole is also a version of the traditional policeman in a thriller: intrusive, commanding, polite but impatient when necessary. The twist in the situation is, of course, that nothing has occurred that would bring any of the family to a court of law. The 'crime' that has been carried out is certainly not a conventional one, no more than the Inspector's manner and questions are conventional. Even Eric's offence – of stealing money from the office – has taken place within the family as it were and appears to us as one of the less serious lapses in the play. Priestley manipulates our sense of what we expect of a policeman/investigator in such a drama and upsets our preconceptions when the Inspector deliberately steps over the normal boundaries imposed in a criminal inquiry.

At times the Inspector plays the voice of conscience. His familiarity with what each member of the household has done goes beyond what any investigator might reasonably be expected to know; things that they have concealed from each other – even from themselves – are brought to the surface at the Inspector's insistence. The Inspector accounts for his knowledge by items found in her room (a letter, a diary) but this merely gives some plausibility to what he knows rather than explaining the sympathy with which he can enter into the circumstances of the life of Eva Smith; Goole is readily able to imagine – and to invite us to imagine – the poverty-stricken desperation of the girl in lodgings.

The Inspector does not know everything about the dead girl or the weaknesses of the Birlings – if he did, he would hardly have a pretext for his inquiry – but we sense that he knows all the essentials of the case. His intimate connection with the Birlings, in which light he might be interpreted as some manifestation of conscious, is suggested by Eric's remark, 'He was our police inspector all right' or Sheila's 'he inspected us all right'.

The Inspector invites the Birlings to do what they have evidently never done before, put themselves in the place of someone who is socially and materially less fortunate than themselves. If Goole is brutal in forcing this awareness on them he is brutal to a purpose – to bring home to this self-satisfied family the real nature of what has happened: 'Her position now is that she lies with a burnt-out inside on a slab.'

The Inspector uncovers the secrets in the Birling household, stops its members from evading responsibility and makes at least two of the characters think and – more importantly – feel differently. He is also given the single most significant statements in the play: 'We are all members of one body. We are responsible for each other.' Priestley throughout gives the Inspector the air of authority which entitles him to carry out a moral rather than a criminal investigation and to make such pronouncements about it. What the other characters have done is variously selfish, mean, jealous, etc., and they respond, according to their natures, with bluster, panic or sorrow. They are judged by the Inspector but he offers neither punishment nor forgiveness to them. The implication is that they must judge themselves and each other. Goole is the catalyst in the Birling house, bringing about some change in all while remaining himself unwaveringly stern and authoritative.

It would be incorrect to suggest that the Inspector stands for some single impersonal force – e.g. conscience or retribution – or appears as the member of some celestial police force. As a character, the Inspector does not change or develop: he does not need to. As with the other characters, Priestley provides a familiar outline to which an audience can respond, but in retrospect the dialogue designed to establish the Inspector's *bona fides* both with Birling and with the audience seems oddly non-committal. Look, for instance, at Goole's evasive responses when Birling attempts to 'place' the Inspector shortly after his entry.

Priestley intentionally leaves the provenance of the figure of the Inspector unexplained, his real identity a mystery. This is more effective than any clarification would have been. To reveal that Goole was, for instance, a practical joker (as the Birlings hope) or that he was some sort of 'avenging spirit' would sacrifice dramatic suggestiveness to precise explanation. As it is, Priestley is able to present on stage the conflict and disturbance that result when a figure of seemingly superhuman – or at any rate non-human – knowledge and power of judgement is introduced into the solid bourgeois reality of an Edwardian household.

Eva Smith

Apart from the maid, Edna, (of no dramatic significance), there is only one other 'character' in *An Inspector Calls*: Eva Smith. Although she never physically appears on stage, her life and death obviously dominate the proceedings and we learn quite a lot about her from the conversations of the other characters. Certain of her attributes are stressed: she was 'lively, good-looking', 'young and fresh and charming', etc. We hear of the events of her life in some detail, especially after she has come into contact with the Birlings. At each encounter Priestley takes care to establish her as the victim of others' selfishness or indifference. In Birling's factory she was 'a good worker', ready for promotion, but in the owner's eye she then became a troublemaker and was sacked for being a strike ring-leader. In fact, the workers' demands are presented as modest; it is the owner who appears unreasonable. At the dress shop her supposed 'impertinence' to Sheila is minimized and it is the Birling daughter who comes out of the affair looking spiteful and petty.

In Acts 2 and 3 the girl becomes the sexual victim of Gerald Croft and of Eric, and pays for her involvement with the latter in Mrs Birling's moralistic rejection of her. Priestley suggests that in her desperation (she is impoverished and 'actually hungry') she is easy prey for the 'respectable' members of the community like Alderman Meggarty. Even her 'rescuer', Gerald, drops her later when he no longer needs her. Despite the suffering and the setbacks she has endured, Eva Smith shows a capacity for finer feeling and better behaviour than any Birling. She turns down the son because he has been stealing money on her behalf, she does not give him away to the mother when she appeals ('alone, friendless, almost penniless, desperate') for help from the charity organization. Finally, and in a horrible manner, she kills both herself and the child she is carrying.

Eva Smith is not a 'character' in the sense that the others are. If she were actually present on stage, for example in a series of flashbacks depicting her gradual ruin, we might find her a rather implausible figure; increasing despair seems to make her more courageous and scrupulous instead of less so. Certainly it would have been a challenge to Priestley as a dramatist to make such a figure credible. In fact, he does not need to do so. Eva Smith appears through the descriptions of the Inspector and others, but our attention is not really concentrated on her; rather we focus on the responses and changes in the characters who have an actual stage life. The girl who commits suicide is a dramatically useful representative of the innocent and the exploited, and because she is so blameless she throws the faults of the Birlings and Gerald Croft into sharper relief.

Themes

The principal theme of *An Inspector Calls* is easily detectable. It is a study of the need for individual and, by extension, for social responsibility. In the words of the character who is the mouthpiece for the author – the Inspector – 'we are members of one body'. The opposing concept to this is self-interest and the character who most explicitly embodies this doctrine is Birling who attacks those idealistic 'cranks' who believe in communal responsibility, the concept that members of a society have some duties and obligations towards each other's welfare. The arrival of the Inspector – and his accusations – heralds the undermining of the complacent and unimaginative philosophy by which the Birlings have conducted their affairs.

The play does not depend, however, upon the vague assertion that one should behave properly towards others because it is the right or 'nice' thing to do. The play's 'message' (to put it crudely) is more rigorous than that. For Priestley demonstrates through the unfolding action of the drama that involvement with other people is inescapable; no element of choice is present. And the fact of involvement, of responsibility, rests particularly heavily on those who choose – or are chosen – to occupy prominent places in society. Priestley indicates that if such responsibilities are ignored or mishandled then disaster is always possible. For example, Birling conceives of his duty in very narrow terms: the maximization of profits. The other side of his responsibility – to his workforce – remains unacknowledged by the factory owner. Birling thinks of labour only in terms of how much 'it' is costing him; when those costs threaten to endanger his profits he acts quickly to avert the danger. Eva Smith, together with a few others, is sacked as an 'agitator' and the process begins that is to enmesh all the members of Birling's family.

Mrs Birling sees the girl as 'impertinent', probably considers her as immoral, certainly identifies her as a member of the lower class with which she will deal only on the narrowest of terms. Her failure of responsibility is both social – she is, after all, in a prominent position in her charity organization and misuses that position to prevent the pregnant girl getting any help – and individual. The Inspector condemns the wilful failure of her sympathy: 'You've had children. You must have known what she was feeling. And you slammed the door in her face.' Similarly, Sheila is convicted by Goole of an abuse of power because she used her financial and social authority to make Eva Smith suffer for a supposed piece of 'mockery' at the dress shop.

Both of the younger men in the play, while not treating Eva Smith with the coldness or callousness of the others, are seen to have dealt with her on their terms and to have consulted their own interests in the affairs. Gerald Croft terminates their liaison when it suits him; endowed with independence because of his money and his social standing, he can afford to move on. Eric emerges in Act 3 as someone who has little control over himself, but the penalty for whose lapses is generally paid for by others. Not one of these characters can escape a knowledge of his or her damaging links to the dead girl – damaging not only to the latter but also to those who have shown insufficient humanity towards her, damaging too to the family bonds (recrimination and abuse replace the family unity shown at the beginning of the play, though it would be possible to argue that such unity was built on lies and misunderstandings and that a greater honesty prevails after the Inspector's call). Priestley's vision – or nightmare – of the ruin that can be brought about by such a wide, communal failure of responsibility extends beyond the confines of a family unit and ultimately embraces society in its widest sense, as we see when the Inspector warns of the self-inflicted suffering that will come if men do not learn the lesson of responsibility.

An Inspector Calls was written in the aftermath of World War II and is set in the years immediately preceding World War I. This provides a deeply ironic context for all the hopeful predictions of progress made at the beginning of the play but it also gives added force and intensity to Priestley's warning. The 'fire and blood and anguish' of the Inspector's warning are the inevitable results of human greed, selfishness and short-sightedness, seen here operating on a domestic level but easily envisioned by an audience as working on a national or global scale.

Of course, wars cannot be attributed directly to small acts of spite or displays of indifference, but human failures of some kind must lie at the bottom of humanly avoidable disasters. Priestley shows that a single act of unkindness may not, by itself, be too dangerous; it is a chain of them which leads to the disaster that finally becomes inevitable. Mistreatment piled on indifference at last brings about the deaths of the girl and her unborn child. And the blame for this is not laid at the door of some abstract concept such as 'society'. Priestley is not providing a critique of the social structure, although the play obviously implies that too much power is in the hands of the 'capitalists' or that power is not used with sufficient awareness of its effects. He does not suggest that some revolutionary change in the system will avert the predicted 'anguish'. The only necessary change – and perhaps it is one harder to bring about than an altered social organization – is a change in human nature. The development of (some of) the characters in the play suggests that such a change is possible though very difficult to accomplish.

A subsidiary theme of the play is an exploration of the effects of guilt. Clearly the characters fall into two groups: those who are too hardened to accept any responsibility for the death of Eva Smith and who attempt to restore things to 'normal' as soon as the Inspector has departed, and those who feel some shame and have begun 'to learn something' from what they have done. The distinction is not entirely produced by a difference in ages between the two groups (Gerald Croft is not much older than Sheila and Eric yet he sides with the Birling parents in Act 3), nor is the division between those who have something to lose through a scandal and those who do not. Sheila and Eric, like the other characters, both have a vested interest in the status quo; the daughter has her engagement to guard while the son has a position in his father's firm which will be compromised by revelations about his drinking and stealing. Both, however, acknowledge the need to confess, to express some regret at what has been done and to consider some future changes. Guilt in them finds an outlet, a process that Priestley suggests is proper and healing.

Guilt in the other characters is suppressed or brushed off. Mr Birling can finally offer 'penitence' but it is couched in the only terms that he understands: 'Look, Inspector – I'd give thousands – yes, thousands –', to which he gets the brisk response, 'You're offering the money at the wrong time'. It is ironic that Birling refused a few shillings to his workers but is now willing to pay 'thousands' to salvage his reputation. But what money could do once it cannot achieve now, and the 'sorrow' that expresses itself exclusively in such material terms shows that Birling is still operating within the narrow terms of imaginative reference that he smugly inhabited at the beginning of the play. Mrs Birling becomes very distressed at the Inspector's final revelations but cannot admit to anything beyond 'I didn't know – I didn't understand'. Eric's reaction to this is, 'You never did. You never even tried –', and we receive elsewhere the impression of Mrs Birling as a cold, aloof woman incapable of responding properly to the needs of others or to the guilt inside herself. The very fact that she recovers self-control soon after the Inspector's exit tells against her. Gerald Croft is upset at the news of Daisy Renton's suicide but rapidly regains his confident manner and can treat his involvement with her in a matter-of-fact way by the end of the play.

Looking at this range of responses, we can see that Priestley could be termed pessimistic – or perhaps just realistic – in his belief in the incapacity of people to show a fundamental charity to each other or even to be aware of the social/moral web that he sees as binding society together. He is also realistic in his depiction of the differing effects of guilt. The play dramatizes the consequences of the failure to recognize one's obligations to others and the process by which those consequences touch not merely those who have been neglected or badly treated but ultimately those responsible for neglect or mistreatment.

These themes are hardly original but that is not the criterion by which their worth and effectiveness can be tested. It is how Priestley deals with the themes that matters, how illuminating and entertaining he succeeds in making the drama that embodies his concerns. To this end, the dramatist adapts a genre (the 'whodunnit' or detective story) which is not noted for the depth of its moral concerns and, without sacrificing the excitement or tension generated by the hunt for a criminal, gives to this old format a more urgent and telling purpose.

An Inspector Calls and its genre

In its structure and partly in its content Priestley's play is indebted to the traditions of detective dramas or 'whodunnits'. The format is familiar both in novels and on the stage. An investigation takes place into a murder, the suspects are limited in number and usually represent stock types. After several false trails have been pursued, the culprit is unmasked through the brilliance and doggedness of the investigator. The principal pleasure for reader or audience usually lies in trying to work out who committed the murder before the detective reveals it. It is not a dramatic genre which has had many outstanding practitioners and the severe limitations of the form – for instance, the need to provide an adequate number of suspects with convincing motives for murder – tend to make for artificiality and contrivance. While the simple 'whodunnit' may never have attracted any great playwrights because the form is unfavourable to any real exploration of human motives or behaviour, elements of the 'detective story' can be found in many profound works (*Hamlet* is an obvious example). Most audiences and readers are familiar with the conventions and associations which belong to the 'whodunnit', a fact exploited by present-day dramatists who have imitated or parodied the genre, for example Tom Stoppard (*The Real Inspector Hound*, 1968) or Anthony Shaffer (*Sleuth*, 1970). Priestley follows a 'whodunnit' author like Agatha Christie in confining his 'suspects' to a restricted community, in this case the Birling family and one outsider. As in a detective story, the characters of those 'suspects' are swiftly established and the arrival of Inspector Goole promises to the audience the enjoyable unmasking of some crime. But this is also the point at which the play departs from the conventional development of a detective story.

There are a number of significant and related differences between *An Inspector Calls* and a 'whodunnit'. The Inspector is not interested in revealing a criminal and then arresting him as the curtain comes down. To begin with, the Birling family has done nothing criminal, in the orthodox sense of the word. At least, the members of that family do not think that any of them has committed a crime. As the evening progresses, however, Inspector Goole forces them to understand that although no crime which could be prosecuted has been perpetrated, a great wrong, nevertheless, has been done by everybody in the household. Whereas the typical thriller proceeds by a process of elimination to reduce the number of suspects until only the guilty party remains, Priestley steers his play in the opposite direction. Guilt and responsibility widen, rather than narrow, until they become communal, even if not accepted by all.

The Inspector is not concerned with punishment in the usual sense. In fact, there is no specific penalty for what the Birlings have done and the worst that hangs over them is the exposure and scandal that would result from an inquest in which their names were brought up (for Mr and Mrs Birling this is a very considerable punishment, even though it is not one laid down by the law). So, in a sense, one could claim that formal 'justice' is not done in this situation, and it is part of the Inspector's remorseless accusation of the family that: 'Eva Smith's gone. You can't do her any more harm. And you can't do her any good now, either. You can't even say "I'm sorry, Eva Smith."' The situation has reached the stage at which any amends have become impossible because the girl is beyond their reach, for good or ill.

The Birlings are also beyond the grasp of the law but are not without the possibility of changing themselves if they wish to. If the Inspector does not threaten them with a specific penalty – though he presents the universal danger of 'fire and blood and anguish' if men do not reform themselves and turn from selfishness and insensitivity – nor does he offer any forgiveness to the 'wrongdoers'. The implication is that each character must both punish and forgive him or herself and live to learn something from the experience. The Inspector suggests ways in which past failings can be redeemed by real charity and the awareness of human interdependence in the future. Sheila demonstrates something of this necessary change when she starts to re-assess her relationship with Gerald Croft.

As in an ordinary 'whodunnit', the author of *An Inspector Calls* is concerned to uncover secrets, responsibility and guilt. Some of the ways in which the unfolding of the plot here diverges from the normal have been indicated above – guilt is general not individual, the Inspector cannot charge anybody with a 'crime' and therefore cannot hold out the prospect of punishment and the restoration of normality through the exercise of justice. The most fundamental difference between Priestley's play and the conventional detective story is that the things that are uncovered by Goole's questioning are not at first seen by those who have done them as wrong or reprehensible. Birling was proud of being a hard-headed businessman who had a no-nonsense way with troublemakers and who thought he could afford to treat people as nothing more than 'cheap labour'. Gerald and Eric were happy enough to use Eva, and although the girl acquiesced in their proposals events make it clear that she came out of each affair at a disadvantage. Furthermore, the relationships involved Gerald in lying to his fiancée and Eric in stealing from Birling & Co. Each man excused these lapses to himself: Gerald eased his conscience by not telling Sheila 'a complete lie when I said I'd been very busy at the works all that time. We were very busy.' Eric claims that the money he had taken was merely 'borrowed'. Both are compelled by the Inspector and others to bring these excuses into the light so that their inadequacy can be seen. Mrs Birling was a self-satisfied member of a charity organization though she failed utterly to show any real charity when put to the test and did 'something terribly wrong' in the Inspector's words or 'cruel and vile' in Sheila's. Sheila herself was quick to abuse her position and influence (as Mrs Birling did hers) in getting the girl sacked for impertinence.

The Inspector shakes their preconceptions about the inevitable rightness of their behaviour. He makes them see — if only momentarily — that what appeared at the time a normal and proper exercise of social, economic or sexual power was in reality a misuse of power, a kind of 'crime'. In other words, Priestley tries to redefine the idea of 'criminal' behaviour so that fairly unexceptional examples of human selfishness and spite become 'offences' for which people can be questioned and brought to account. In the process the barrier between bad but 'legal' actions and bad but 'illegal' ones is broken down. Gerald Croft, like the Birlings, is confident of his respectability as a citizen, but the Inspector suggests that the line between innocence and wrong-doing is very hard to establish.

Priestley suggests that there are laws other than the laws of the land which may be broken and that, although these laws may not be codified in the statute books, to break them can bring penalties which lie outside the resources of the courts but which are none the less real. The punishment for those insensitive to anybody's feelings but their own is the loss of reputation, the punishment for the more receptive in the Birling family — Sheila and Eric — is self-reproach, an inescapable awareness that the crime each has committed has to be atoned for in some way.

The Inspector's questions shake the family, just as the action of the play as a whole is meant to stimulate the audience into some recognition of the nature of human and social responsibility. But Priestley is not producing a tract, he is creating a moral entertainment; he employs and manipulates the 'whodunnit' formula because the inquisitorial method of discovery used by the detective is a dramatically exciting way of bringing to light what is a moral rather than a legal truth. He also employs it because the pattern of question, answer and discovery is an intrinsically satisfying process for the audience to see.

In the conventional detective story such patterns are put at the service of a puzzle and the underlying assumptions of such a story are left unexamined – for example, there is never any doubt over what is or is not criminal behaviour. The 'puzzle' for Priestley, however, is the rather deeper mystery of human nature and how to bring people to a truer acknowledgement of themselves and of others. The answer for the playwright is not the easy solution where the criminal is taken away for punishment and the world made safe again, as in the formula drama. The 'solution' in *An Inspector Calls* is tentatively offered and perhaps idealistic: it is that, to avert disaster, people must behave better. The 'villain' is more easily detectable than is usual in the 'whodunnit'; the guilty party is the entire family, and the members of it can either confess to the 'crime' or evasively attempt to acquit themselves. There is no doubt as to which Priestley thinks is the better course.

Dramatic structure

An Inspector Calls follows what are sometimes called the dramatic unities. These concepts, deriving in part from the Greek philosopher Aristotle, are to be found more often in theory than in practice but Priestley provides a text-book example of them in this play. The unities are: that a play should consist of one action (i.e. no sub-plot), should take place in one setting and should occupy roughly the same amount of time as the events depicted on stage would take if they were occurring in reality. Without any sense of strain Priestley fulfils these conditions. There is only one plot in *An Inspector Calls*: everything that happens after Goole's entry is governed by the family's complicity in the death of Eva Smith. There is only one setting (the Birlings' dining-room) and the passing of time as experienced by the characters on stage is identical to the audience's experience, the only breaks being for two intervals, and at the end of each of these the action resumes at precisely the point at which it was broken at the conclusion of the preceding act. Observance of these 'unities' would generally tend to enhance the realism or naturalism of a drama. After making an initial acceptance of the situation depicted in a play, the audience is not required to make any subsequent adjustments, as it must when the setting of the play undergoes a geographical shift (as in *Othello*, for example, where the scene shifts from Venice to Cyprus) or when the action jumps across a long period of time (Shakespeare again provides an instance of this when the action of *The Winter's Tale* skips across sixteen years at one bound). In practice, an audience is usually prepared to accept the conditions a dramatist imposes upon it, whether these include shifts of time and space or not. However, for a playwright working within the conventions of naturalism – as Priestley is in this play (with the exception of the surprise ending which adds a non-realistic dimension to the drama) – there are obvious attractions in presenting a version of events on stage which comes as close as possible to recreating the circumstances of real life. From this concentration of time, place and action Priestley gains an intensity which would be lessened if, say, the action were spread over several days or several scenes.

The gains of setting a play in one time and one place may become drawbacks if dramatic momentum is not maintained and the play acquires a static quality. The principal necessity is to provide fresh and exciting developments in narrative and character without sacrificing plausibility. Priestley succeeds in this. Although the pattern of discovery and guilt in the Birling family is perceivable from an early point in the action – certainly by the end of Act 1 – there are other elements in narrative and character development which hold an audience's attention.

There is, first, the life-story of Eva Smith; the Inspector provides the framework for this story, above all the knowledge of how the girl died, while the Birlings provide the details. Goole is both narrator and inquirer – he is on a moral quest to lay the blame for the suicide where it belongs, but there is also in his questioning a simple desire to find out what happened, and he communicates this desire to the audience. He speaks for that audience when he says, 'I said to myself:

"Well, we'll try to understand why it had to happen." And that's why I'm here, and why I'm not going until I know *all* that happened.'

Notice that here the Inspector implicitly denies the overall knowledge that Sheila credits him with, and of course if he did know everything already he would be deprived of the pretext for his inquiry. Indeed the audience would be without the simple but important satisfaction of hearing the unfolding history of Eva Smith.

Another way of maintaining the audience's interest is to ensure that the reactions of the Birlings and Gerald Croft to what they have done are as different as possible. As stated above, we realize fairly soon that everybody is going to have to explain his or her involvement with the dead girl, that all of them are implicated. But we do not know how (narrative development) and we do not know the way in which each person on stage will respond individually (character development). The situation grows more complex as the characters not only reveal something about themselves by the way in which they react to the Inspector's questions but also respond to each other: each sees him or herself in a new light (or tries to avoid that painful necessity) as well as coming to judge the others differently.

Because Priestley is working within a familiar genre and because the pattern of discovery and guilt in the Birling family quickly establishes its own momentum, the author has to strive both to satisfy an audience's legitimate expectations and to avoid predictability. Dramatic structure is obviously paramount here. Act 3 is a good example of Priestley's skill in ordering what happens on stage in such a way as to sustain audience interest and provide a satisfying dramatic 'shape'.

The Inspector's condemnation of the Birlings rises to a height, he exits and a period of recrimination begins; then relief, as they start to realize that he was not a genuine policeman. So far the audience will – if Priestley's drama has worked – have felt something of the force of the Inspector's warning but also something of the family's relief. It is not inconsistent to feel with both 'sides' in a dramatic conflict; in fact it is a necessary feature of a play's effectiveness that one should be enabled by the dramatist to enter the emotions and ideas of each of the opposing groups, even if only briefly. We follow the steps by which it is revealed that Goole was an impostor and the mechanics of this discovery are quite absorbing, from Sheila's doubts to the first of the telephone calls made by Mr Birling. As the family complacency sets in again, so should the audience's indignation rise to echo Sheila's protest that, even if the suicide has not occurred, the other events have taken place; escape from the final tragedy is no cause for self-congratulation in the family.

Then Priestley engineers a surprise reversal of events. What appeared to be serious and then an elaborate practical joke turns out to be serious after all. The final telephone call from the police proves that. Whatever the real identity of Inspector Goole, the connections that he established between this smug household and the dead girl were true enough and they are about to be pored over again by a genuine police inspector as the play ends. This conclusion is satisfying in several ways. It completes – or at least continues – a pattern: the play appears to have gone full circle, ending where it began (with an inspector's call) but with some of the characters better or worse than they were at the start. The ending also answers the audience's tacit demand for justice or fairness: the Birlings are not going to 'get away with it', they will not be allowed to resume their normal lives as if nothing had happened.

We do not need to see the probable chain of events which would follow the appearance of a genuine policeman after the play's end. From what we already know of the characters we can envisage the honesty of some, the continued evasions of others.

Certainly the scandal of which the Birling parents are so frightened will follow. But the ending of *An Inspector Calls* is not just a *coup de théâtre*. Priestley here harmonizes the moral import of his work with structure. The ending is a fitting punishment for the Birlings. Sheila and Eric apart, they have not taken seriously the Inspector's 'lesson'; instead they begin to disclaim responsibility as soon as Goole has left, and attempt to place the blame elsewhere. They have learned nothing so the process of accusation and self-examination will have to be gone through all over again. The defences – of self-deception and excuse – that have been hurriedly raised will be demolished again and the worldly penalty, of exposure and scandal, will be exacted, as the final stage direction indicates: '*they stare guiltily and dumbfounded.*'

In this discussion of structure it should also be noted that two aspects of *An Inspector Calls* reflect Priestley's life-long interest in the relationship between time and human experience, precognition and 'repetition'. The Inspector's knowledge of the girl's death can only be attributed to precognition on his part, i.e. he knows about this event before it has taken place. This point is explicitly made at the end of the play: when Gerald telephones the Infirmary he finds out that they have not had a suicide case; moments later Birling receives the call which says that 'a girl has just died – on her way to the Infirmary'. At about the same time, therefore, as they are congratulating each other on their lucky escape, their 'victim' is dying but this occurs *after* the Inspector's visit. Other of Priestley's plays exhibit a similar interest in precognition or foreknowledge, e.g. *Time and the Conways* (1937) and *I Have Been Here Before* (1937). In fact, precognition is not a central element of *An Inspector Calls*. Priestley is not mounting an investigation into the nature of time, as he does elsewhere. Goole's awareness of Eva Smith's death before it has occurred introduces a supernatural – or at least non-rational – note into the play's closing moments. This gives a collective 'thrill' to the audience and provides an appropriate moment for the curtain to drop; it also suggests that Goole has origins or resources which are beyond the merely human.

The other notion connected with time in this play is that of 'repetition', that events may recur. Priestley employed a similar trick of repetition in the very first play he wrote, *Dangerous Corner* (1932), where events which have unfolded in the course of the action appear set to repeat themselves at the end until a lucky accident starts the characters travelling in a different direction. In

An Inspector Calls it is evident that nothing will intervene to prevent the Birlings being subjected to a renewed interrogation of their involvement with Eva Smith. In other plays Priestley holds out the prospect of an escape from the limitations of time; some characters rise above the narrow temporal horizon. In this play there is no escape, and the circularity of the play's construction would seem designed to reinforce Priestley's message that we cannot avoid the consequences of our actions.

Another important aspect of dramatic structure is the possibilities it provides to the playwright for the employment of irony. *An Inspector Calls* offers many examples of irony, both general and particular. There is the irony, easily perceived by the audience, of Birling's confidence in the future, exemplified by his comments about the Titanic or the impossibility of war with the Germans. The function of such moments is to establish his obtuseness as a character, his capacity to overlook what he does not want to know. More generally, the complacency and self-congratulation of the family party at the beginning of Act 1 acquire ironic overtones in retrospect as we learn how unjustified such feelings are. An experienced audience, in fact, would not have to wait to discover that the author was being ironic in his depiction of such characters: the very excess of their smugness and sureness appears to demand an ironic reversal. There is individual irony. Sheila's protest to her father, 'But these girls aren't cheap labour – they're *people*', indicates her ready sympathy, but our sense of her worth as a character is qualified when we find out that she has indeed treated the same girl as a disposable piece of 'cheap labour' in getting her dismissed from the dress shop. Mrs Birling's confident entry and her arrogant comments at the beginning of Act 2 are likewise ironic because we know that her self-assurance is misplaced and that the Inspector will shortly establish a link between herself and the dead girl. Priestley maximizes the irony at the end of this act by making the mother unknowingly condemn her absent son in the strongest terms, just as she has already unknowingly condemned her unborn grandchild by turning away Eva Smith from her 'charity' organization.

Priestley is not of course using irony to mock his creations but to show the inadequacy of their outlook and responses. Unconscious spoken irony depends upon the speaker's ignorance of circumstances or unawareness of what he or she is revealing;

for instance, Mrs Birling's comment about the Inspector, 'The rude way he spoke to Mr Birling and me — it was quite extraordinary!', is ironic because of what she unconsciously reveals about her scale of values (that the policeman's supposed bluntness is more offensive to her than the whole business of the suicide) and because the word 'extraordinary' could more properly be applied to her own behaviour than Inspector Goole's. One could find many other such examples of irony in the play, and Priestley enlarges the scope for it by arranging the entry of the Birlings before the Inspector in such a way as to prevent each of them knowing too much about what has been revealed of Eva Smith's life and death prior to his or her entry. Sheila and Eric attack their father over his treatment of his workers before realizing their own guilt; Gerald imagines he has no part in 'this suicide business'; Mrs Birling's arrogant detachment has already been mentioned. With some skill Priestley manipulates the entrances and exits of his characters so that he achieves dramatic impact from the irony which is based on ignorance of circumstances or, more profoundly, ignorance of the self. The Birlings and Gerald Croft see themselves as worthy citizens, principled upholders of moral rectitude; we see them differently. In the gap between their perception of themselves and our understanding of them is the fertile ground for irony.

It should therefore be apparent that the structure of *An Inspector Calls* is of paramount importance in any discussion of the play's success. The manipulation of events on stage, of characters, the ordering of time and space, serve the ultimate purpose of holding the audience's interest, rousing its emotions and thoughts. Priestley ensures that our attention is fastened on the play by variations in tempo and mood — from complacency to anxiety and fear, followed by a partial return to a complacency undermined by a final revelation; by his use of irony in which the audience is often in a kind of conspiracy with the author; and by his confident use of the techniques of naturalism by which Priestly lulls us into a false sense of security so that the ending — with its suggestions of 'other worldliness' — is that much more effective.

Language

The style of the language of *An Inspector Calls* corresponds to the play's surface realism. All the characters employ colloquial English in their dialogue and there is no attempt at the kind of stylized or 'poetic' prose which Priestley sometimes introduces into other dramas. The characters also inhabit the same social plane so there is no variation in diction or syntax. Priestley does however differentiate between his characters by giving them dialogue appropriate to age or temperament. The comparative youth and spontaneity of Eric and Sheila are suggested by a little (period) slang: terms such as 'chump', 'squiffy', 'ass' all help to distinguish the Birling children from their parents and the use of such minor linguistic details enables Priestley to set the play in its historical context as well as to suggest the greater freedom – of outlook, of language – enjoyed by Sheila and Eric.

By contrast the speech of the Birling parents is calculated and self-conscious. Mr Birling is expansive and opinionated at the beginning of the play – he can talk down to those who have less knowledge of the world than himself. The two states of mind suggested by Birling's words and actions throughout the play are self-satisfaction and panic. In between is a matter-of-fact determination, well shown by the terse and clipped style of his account of the strike at his factory and its aftermath:

I told the girl to clear out, and she went. That's the last I heard of her. Have you any idea what happened to her after that? Get into trouble? Go on the streets?

Mrs Birling takes longer to break down than her husband; her self-righteousness and inflexibility give her an almost impenetrable armour to ward off the Inspector's accusations. But if her speech is decisive and imperious Priestley matches it with the authoritative manner of the Inspector. From the moment he enters Goole creates an impression of 'solidity and purposefulness' (see stage direction); he never wavers in his determination to uncover the truth and his speech has an easy confidence which compels the Birlings to attend to what he is saying. Goole moves from relaxed narration to rebuke and judgement, as one sees throughout the play. When Birling delivers his opinions to Eric and Gerald Croft at the beginning of the play we reject what he is saying because of the shallow complacency of his words; we accept the Inspector's judgements partly because the play demonstrates the rightness of what he is saying and partly because they are couched in terms which suggest the common sense and common decency which Priestley tacitly assumes his audiences will share with him. The connection between the Inspector and his creator is close. There are moments in the play when Goole talks with an unforced, unpompous sympathy – or anger – which recall Priestley's manner of writing in his own person.

Priestley's dialogue is serviceable rather than memorable but we should note the way in which character outlines are sharpened by small differences in speech.

Setting

The setting of *An Inspector Calls* is the Birlings' house in Brumley, an imaginary name but one easily enough identified with one of the major Midlands centres of population and industry such as Birmingham. The time is a spring evening in 1912.

Some of Priestley's reasons for setting the play in this period have been mentioned in earlier sections. The years in Britain preceding World War I are generally described as the Edwardian age or era, though in fact the king after whom they are named (Edward VII) had died in 1910, to be succeeded by George V. With hindsight this pre-war period appeared to be a time of security and prosperity although whether it was actually experienced as such by the majority of the population must be very doubtful. A minority – the class to which Birling belongs – did well but the mass – represented by Eva Smith and the other girls at Birling's factory – was badly paid, vulnerable to exploitation at work, largely unprotected by unions or by the state. At the same time there was a large and increasing group of workers who fitted into neither category, the suburban and white-collar middle class, but Priestley is concerned to show the social extremes rather than the group in the middle.

Some idea of the social and economic divisions is conveyed by the fact that just before the outbreak of World War I the average wage for a male industrial worker was £75 a year. (The pay that Eva Smith receives, on the figures supplied by Birling in Act 1, is less than £60 a year. The increase for which she and her fellow workers go on strike is about another £6 a year). The average annual income of someone earning a salary, that is, of someone belonging to the middle class with secure employment, was over four times the amount paid to the factory hand. Birling, of course, as an employer on a large scale, would be a wealthy man and he would not be constrained by much in his treatment of his workers. Women were paid worse than men but would be just as desperate for employment if unsupported (Eva Smith's parents are dead); there was little social provision for those who did not help themselves and charity was left largely to organizations like Mrs Birling's committee. Over the heads of any workers who grew troublesome Mr Birling could hold the threat that: 'if they didn't like those rates (of pay), they could go and work somewhere else. It's a free country, I told them.' There is no net to catch Eva Smith when she falls; she has to depend on the very questionable charity of those she encounters on the way down. One of Priestley's reasons, therefore, in setting the play at this particular historical time is that the decline of a figure like Eva Smith from poorly paid employment to destitution can be more plausibly presented than it could have been at a later period when social legislation lessened some of the worst effects of poverty and unemployment.

Similarly the siting of the play's action in a comfortable house in an industrial city has a relevance to the author's chosen period. In the early years of the twentieth century Britain was the leading industrial power in the world, although her dominance in this field was threatened by both America and Germany. In the great industrial centres of the Midlands and the North the products were manufactured to be exported round the world just as other less material products of Britain (law, government etc.) had already been exported throughout the British Empire. In reality it was a considerably less healthy and rosy picture than it looked. Industrially, Britain was about to be overtaken; the British Empire, as well as other power blocs in Europe, would start to fall apart sooner than anyone expected; there was anxiety about war with Germany (dismissed by Birling and indirectly referred to by the Inspector); and there was obviously a growing concern about the kind of social conditions that caused a large proportion of the population to live inadequately in material terms while the minority enjoyed a pleasant prosperity (Eric and Sheila touch on this subject when they object to their father's treatment of his factory workers). However, on the surface things looked well enough, and growth and prosperity seemed assured, as we see from Birling's comments in the early part of the play. Birling's views must have been representative of the views of many comfortably situated men like himself. What happens in *An Inspector Calls* shows up the defects in the Birlings' view of the world and, although Priestley is not writing a political tract in which the shortcomings of the ruling class or the long-suffering of the working class are offered in ideological terms, we can see that some criticism is being made of a system which encourages such divisions between the groups which make up an industrial society.

From a narrative aspect, setting the story in a city provides a more emphatic context for Eva Smith's loneliness and destitution. As Birling is a representative of a type of employer, so is the girl only one of many others in similar circumstances. An industrial centre will draw many people from outside with the prospect of jobs – Eva Smith is 'country-bred' – but will not provide anything if those jobs fail. A place of the size and importance of Brumley, significant enough to be visited by Royalty, as Birling mentions in connection with his hoped-for knighthood, will also have a hierarchy to which its more worthy citizens will belong or aspire. The Birling parents are proud of their position and titles – ex-Lord Mayor, magistrate etc. – as well as the fact that they are on close terms with other influential members of the community like the Chief Constable. Priestley suggests that the failings and double standards of the Birlings and Gerald Croft extend throughout the Brumley 'establishment'. The other side of 'respectability' is hypocrisy and scandal which must remain secret or, if known about, cannot be openly acknowledged because the pretensions of people like the Birlings to moral, as well as economic and social superiority, will be destroyed. Outwardly high standards are still frequently expected in 'public' figures but the setting and period of *An Inspector Calls* recall a time when those standards were less flexible and when the penalty for being seen to fall beneath them was harsher than it is at the present day.

General questions plus questions on related topics for coursework/examination on other books you may be studying

1 What are the essentials of Mr Birling's character and what changes do we see in him in the course of the play?

Suggested notes for essay answer:

Basically unattractive figure, snob satisfied with own position and that of his family. Successful businessman 'hard-headed, practical'. Complacently certain of 'peace and prosperity and rapid progress everywhere' as he is sure of the unassailable rightness of his behaviour. Socially a little uneasy in presence of Gerald Croft because latter comes from a 'better' family 'landed people and so forth' but he finds some consolation in the prospect of a knighthood. Also gets reassurance from his social position and 'titles' which he is ready to use as a weapon to put others in their place.

At first justifies behaviour without too much discomfort but tone changes when he discovers that the Inspector has not come to see him alone but other members of his family. He is 'protective' but in the wrong way – wants to prevent Sheila hearing indelicate details of Gerald's involvement, responds angrily when Goole accuses his wife of not telling truth. Only moved by thought of scandal and how it will affect him; personally outraged by revelation that Eric stole from '*my* office' because this hits him in a vulnerable spot (concern for money) and because it is a piece of personal betrayal by his son.

Does not receive Inspector's warning – after latter's exit turns on son to make scapegoat of him – no attempt to face up to reality of what all have done nor to bind up family wounds. He and Mrs Birling leap eagerly on Gerald's interpretation of events which allows them a way out from exposure and social embarrassment. Oblivious to his children's appeals that whole business cannot be shrugged off so easily; once everything seems 'all right' he quickly resumes surface hardness and bluffness that have protected him so far. But there is something bogus about his good humour at the end as there is about his complacency at the beginning of the play. Birling does not really change during course of play but the essential hollowness of his character is revealed.

2 What advantages are gained from setting *An Inspector Calls* within a confined space and time?

3 How does the early presentation of Sheila and Eric in the play prepare us for their later responses to Eva Smith's death?

4 Would it be true to say that Mrs Birling is an utterly unsympathetic figure?

5 'You and I aren't the same people who sat down to dinner here.' What changes does Gerald Croft undergo throughout the play?

6 Discuss the different concepts of the word 'duty' as used in the play.

7 'But he made us confess.' How did Inspector Goole make the Birlings and Gerald Croft 'confess'?

8 Provide and discuss examples from the text which suggest that the Inspector is a genuine policeman together with the evidence that his role stretches beyond this.

9 How would you answer the criticism that Eva Smith is an impossibly idealized figure?

10 Which character emerges least well from his or her involvement with Eva Smith? Give reasons for your choice.

11 Why does Priestley reserve Eric's 'confession' until the last?

12 'But the whole thing's different now,' says Birling when he believes that his family has been fooled by an imposter. Explain why some characters believe that everything has been changed by this discovery while others believe that nothing is different in essentials.

13 How does Priestley extend the themes of the play so that what he says is applicable to a society as much as to a family?

14 How does Priestley manipulate the audience's responses in the final act?

15 'Inspector Goole is not so much a character as a symbol.' Discuss.

16 'What girl? There were probably four or five different girls.' Why does Gerald Croft make this claim and what difference would it make if it were true?

17 What do you find technically ingenious in *An Inspector Calls*?

18 How would you answer the charge that Priestley relies too heavily on stock characters and dialogue?

19 If you were directing *An Inspector Calls* on stage what opportunities and problems might you encounter?

20 Try to account for the continued popularity of *An Inspector Calls*.

21 Discuss the relationship between the various members of the family in *An Inspector Calls*. Compare with another text that deals with a family in crisis (such as *Spring and Port Wine*).

22 Write a short scene following on from the point at which Priestley closes the action in Act 3 until the moment when the real Inspector arrives. Convey your understanding of the characters, paying particular attention to any changes they have undergone in the course of the action.

23 Would you agree that *An Inspector Calls* shows that justice is hard to obtain? Look at other texts which deal with this topic — for example, *To Kill a Mockingbird*.

24 'In *An Inspector Calls* Priestley shows the indifference of those with power to those without it; the Inspector's words on social responsibility in the third Act clearly foreshadow the great wars of the twentieth century.' Use any reading you have done in the literature of the First World War (poets such as Wilfred Owen or Siegfried Sassoon, the drama *Journey's End*) and examine the accuracy of this statement.

25 How far is *An Inspector Calls* like a conventional detective story or 'whodunnit'? In what important respects is it different?

26 Imagine that you are the real police inspector whose arrival is imminent at the end of the play. Write a 'report' of your questioning of the Birling family. Bring out the differences between the various members of the family, and indicate whether there is any 'crime' they might be charged with.

27 Write some entries for Eva Smith's diary covering any of the events referred to in the play. Bring out what you know about her and about those she meets.

28 Compare the structure of *An Inspector Calls* to that of another play you have studied. Look at the way characters are introduced, the point at which scenes or acts are concluded, the way tension is maintained.

29 How much do the setting (one room in a prosperous household) and the references to a particular period (1912) contribute to *An Inspector Calls*? Compare with another drama set in a single location (e.g. *Journey's End, The Long, The Short and The Tall, Spring and Port Wine*).

30 Show how emotional conflict is at the root of this drama, and introduce examples of similar conflict between groups or individuals from at least two other texts which you have read.

Further reading

Any comprehensive history of the British theatre in the twentieth century includes mention of Priestley, generally categorizing him as a writer of comedies and experimental drama.

J. B. Priestley – The Dramatist, Gareth Lloyd Evans (Heinemann, 1964). This is a full account of Priestley's attitude to the theatre and of his total dramatic output and contains a brief analysis of *An Inspector Calls*.

J. B. Priestley: The Last of The Sages, John Atkins (Calder, 1981). Contains comments on the play under study.